EMMANUEL JOSEPH

The Celestial Narrative, How Stars and Stories Shape Our Psychological Landscape

Copyright © 2025 by Emmanuel Joseph

All rights reserved. No part of this publication may be reproduced, stored or transmitted in any form or by any means, electronic, mechanical, photocopying, recording, scanning, or otherwise without written permission from the publisher. It is illegal to copy this book, post it to a website, or distribute it by any other means without permission.

First edition

This book was professionally typeset on Reedsy.
Find out more at reedsy.com

Contents

1	Chapter 1: The Dawn of Celestial Fascination	1
2	Chapter 2: Myth and Magic: The Power of Star Stories	3
3	Chapter 3: The Stars as Guiding Lights	5
4	Chapter 4: The Celestial Influence on Art and Literature	6
5	Chapter 5: The Stars in Modern Psychology	8
6	Chapter 6: The Stars and Human Emotion	10
7	Chapter 7: Celestial Symbolism in Dreams	11
8	Chapter 8: The Stars and Cultural Identity	12
9	Chapter 9: Celestial Bodies and Personal Growth	14
10	Chapter 10: The Therapeutic Power of Stargazing	16
11	Chapter 11: Celestial Archetypes and the Collective...	18
12	Chapter 12: The Future of Our Celestial Narrative	20
13	Chapter 13: Star Symbolism in Religion and Spirituality	22
14	Chapter 14: The Role of Astronomy in Human Progress	23
15	Chapter 15: The Future of Our Celestial Connection	24

1

Chapter 1: The Dawn of Celestial Fascination

From time immemorial, humans have gazed at the night sky, captivated by the brilliance of the stars. These twinkling lights have not only sparked our curiosity but have also inspired countless myths, legends, and stories. The celestial bodies served as the first canvas upon which early humans projected their hopes, fears, and dreams. This chapter delves into the origins of our fascination with the stars, tracing back to ancient civilizations and their interpretations of the cosmos.

Ancient Egyptians, for example, believed that the stars were the souls of the dead, and their constellations were gods watching over them. The Greeks, on the other hand, saw the stars as a way to understand the will of the gods, using astrology to predict future events. These early interpretations of the night sky laid the foundation for our psychological connection to the stars, intertwining our stories with the celestial.

As societies evolved, so did their understanding and narrative of the stars. With advancements in astronomy, the celestial bodies were no longer seen as mere spiritual entities but as objects that could be studied and understood. This shift in perspective did not diminish the stories but rather enriched them, blending scientific discovery with age-old myths. The stars continued to serve as a mirror to our collective psyche, reflecting our quest for knowledge and meaning.

Today's fascination with the cosmos is a testament to our enduring connection with the stars. From the awe-inspiring images captured by telescopes to the imaginative stories crafted in science fiction, the celestial narrative remains a powerful influence on our psychological landscape. As we continue to explore the universe, we are reminded of the profound impact the stars have on our lives, shaping our understanding of the world and our place within it.

2

Chapter 2: Myth and Magic: The Power of Star Stories

Throughout history, myths and legends surrounding the stars have held a significant place in shaping human culture and psychology. These stories served as a means to explain the unexplainable, providing comfort and understanding in a vast and mysterious universe. The constellations, in particular, became a tapestry of tales, each star a character in a grand celestial narrative.

In ancient Greece, the constellation of Orion was seen as a mighty hunter, while the Pleiades were the seven sisters pursued by him. These stories were not just entertainment but also served as moral lessons and guides for navigating life. The stars became a way to encode cultural values and wisdom, passed down through generations in the form of captivating tales.

The power of star stories lies in their ability to transcend time and space, connecting us to our ancestors and future generations. These narratives have a unique way of resonating with our deepest emotions, tapping into our fears, hopes, and desires. By personifying the stars, we create a bridge between the celestial and the terrestrial, allowing us to make sense of our place in the universe.

Even in modern times, the magic of star stories endures. The rise of space exploration and advancements in astrophysics have not diminished our love for these tales. Instead, they have provided new material for storytelling, blending scientific knowledge with imaginative fiction. The stars continue to inspire us, fueling our creativity and shaping our psychological landscape in profound ways.

3

Chapter 3: The Stars as Guiding Lights

For millennia, the stars have served as navigational aids, guiding travelers across vast oceans and deserts. This practical use of celestial bodies has also left a lasting psychological imprint, symbolizing guidance, hope, and the pursuit of one's destiny. The North Star, or Polaris, has been a beacon for sailors and explorers, representing a constant and reliable point in an ever-changing world.

The psychological impact of the stars as guiding lights extends beyond physical navigation. They have come to symbolize our inner journey, guiding us through the uncertainties and challenges of life. In literature and art, the metaphor of the stars as a guiding force is a recurring theme, reflecting our innate desire for direction and purpose.

In times of hardship and uncertainty, the stars offer a sense of stability and hope. During the dark nights of war, refugees and soldiers alike have looked to the night sky for comfort and reassurance. The stars remind us that no matter how chaotic life may seem, there is always a constant presence watching over us, guiding us through the storm.

The stars as guiding lights continue to influence our psychological landscape, inspiring us to seek out our own paths and destinies. Whether we are navigating the physical world or the complexities of our inner selves, the celestial bodies offer a sense of direction and hope, reminding us that we are part of something greater than ourselves.

4

Chapter 4: The Celestial Influence on Art and Literature

The stars have long been a source of inspiration for artists and writers, their brilliance and mystery fueling the creative process. From Van Gogh's "Starry Night" to Shakespeare's references to the cosmos, the celestial bodies have left an indelible mark on the world of art and literature. This chapter explores how the stars have shaped human creativity, leaving a lasting impact on our cultural and psychological landscape.

In visual art, the depiction of the stars has evolved over time, reflecting our changing understanding of the cosmos. Ancient cave paintings of star patterns give way to Renaissance masterpieces that blend scientific observation with artistic expression. The stars in art serve as a bridge between the known and the unknown, inviting viewers to explore the mysteries of the universe.

Literature, too, has been profoundly influenced by the stars. Poets and novelists have long turned to the night sky for inspiration, using celestial imagery to convey emotions and themes. The stars become symbols of love, fate, and the infinite, their presence in literature a testament to their enduring power over the human psyche.

The celestial influence on art and literature continues to thrive in modern times. Contemporary artists and writers draw on the vastness of the cosmos

CHAPTER 4: THE CELESTIAL INFLUENCE ON ART AND LITERATURE

to explore new ideas and push creative boundaries. The stars remain a source of wonder and inspiration, shaping our cultural narrative and enriching our psychological landscape.

5

Chapter 5: The Stars in Modern Psychology

In modern psychology, the stars and their stories continue to play a significant role in shaping our understanding of the human mind. The concept of "star psychology" explores how celestial bodies influence our thoughts, emotions, and behaviors. This chapter delves into the various ways in which the stars intersect with psychological theories and practices.

Astrology, for instance, has long been a tool for understanding personality and predicting future events. While its scientific validity is debated, astrology's influence on popular culture and individual psychology is undeniable. Many people find comfort and guidance in their horoscopes, using the stars as a framework for making sense of their lives.

Beyond astrology, the stars also serve as metaphors in psychological practices. Therapists often use celestial imagery to help clients navigate their inner worlds, guiding them through the darkness to find their own "guiding star." The stars become symbols of hope and resilience, reminding us that even in the darkest times, there is light to be found.

The study of the stars in modern psychology also intersects with existential and transpersonal theories. The vastness of the cosmos invites us to contemplate our place in the universe, leading to profound questions about existence and purpose. This existential exploration can be both daunting and

CHAPTER 5: THE STARS IN MODERN PSYCHOLOGY

inspiring, offering a unique perspective on the human condition.

6

Chapter 6: The Stars and Human Emotion

The stars have a profound impact on our emotions, evoking a sense of awe, wonder, and connection. This chapter explores the emotional responses elicited by the night sky and how they shape our psychological landscape. From the joy of stargazing to the melancholy of contemplating the infinite, the stars have a unique ability to touch our hearts and minds.

The awe and wonder inspired by the stars are rooted in their beauty and mystery. Gazing at the night sky, we are reminded of the vastness of the universe and our small place within it. This sense of awe can be both humbling and uplifting, fostering a deeper appreciation for the world around us.

Stargazing also has a calming effect on the mind, offering a moment of peace and reflection. In a fast-paced and stressful world, the stars provide a sense of tranquility and perspective. Many people find solace in the night sky, using it as a way to unwind and reconnect with themselves.

The emotional impact of the stars is not limited to positive feelings. The contemplation of the infinite can also evoke feelings of existential anxiety and melancholy. The vastness of the cosmos can be overwhelming, leading to questions about our purpose and significance. However, these emotions can also be a source of growth, prompting us to seek deeper meaning and connection.

7

Chapter 7: Celestial Symbolism in Dreams

The stars often appear in our dreams, serving as powerful symbols of our subconscious mind. This chapter explores the significance of celestial imagery in dreams and how it shapes our psychological landscape. From dreams of flying among the stars to nightmares of falling into the void, the night sky reflects our innermost thoughts and emotions.

Dreams of stars often symbolize hope, inspiration, and the pursuit of goals. The stars represent our aspirations and desires, guiding us toward our dreams. These dreams can be motivating and empowering, encouraging us to reach for the stars in our waking lives.

Conversely, nightmares involving the stars can reflect our fears and anxieties. The vastness of the cosmos can be intimidating, evoking feelings of isolation and insignificance. These dreams often mirror our struggles and insecurities, prompting us to confront and address them.

The interpretation of celestial symbolism in dreams is deeply personal and can vary from individual to individual. However, the common theme is that the stars serve as a mirror to our subconscious, reflecting our innermost thoughts and emotions. By exploring these dreams, we can gain valuable insights into our psychological landscape and navigate our inner world.

8

Chapter 8: The Stars and Cultural Identity

The stars have played a significant role in shaping cultural identities around the world. This chapter examines how different cultures have interpreted and incorporated celestial bodies into their narratives, influencing their psychological landscape.

The Indigenous peoples of Australia, for instance, have a deep connection to the stars, incorporating them into their Dreamtime stories and cultural practices. The constellations are seen as ancestral beings, each star telling a story that is woven into the fabric of their cultural identity. This celestial narrative provides a sense of continuity and belonging, connecting individuals to their ancestors and the land.

Similarly, the Inca civilization in South America used the stars to mark important events and agricultural cycles. The alignment of certain constellations with the landscape was believed to signify the presence of their gods, guiding their daily lives and cultural practices. The celestial bodies became integral to their identity, shaping their understanding of the world and their place within it.

In modern times, the stars continue to influence cultural identity, particularly in the realm of space exploration. The achievements of space-faring nations become sources of national pride and identity, inspiring generations to look to the stars with hope and ambition. The shared goal of exploring the cosmos unites people across cultures, fostering a sense of global identity

CHAPTER 8: THE STARS AND CULTURAL IDENTITY

and cooperation.

The stars' impact on cultural identity highlights the profound connection between the celestial and the terrestrial. By examining the ways in which different cultures interpret and incorporate the stars into their narratives, we gain a deeper understanding of the psychological landscape and the universal themes that bind humanity.

9

Chapter 9: Celestial Bodies and Personal Growth

The stars have long been symbols of personal growth and transformation, guiding individuals on their journeys of self-discovery. This chapter explores how the celestial bodies inspire and influence our psychological development, shaping our understanding of ourselves and our potential.

The metaphor of reaching for the stars is a powerful symbol of aspiration and ambition. The stars represent our highest goals and dreams, encouraging us to strive for excellence and push beyond our limits. This pursuit of the stars can be both motivating and challenging, prompting us to confront our fears and embrace our potential.

Celestial imagery also plays a significant role in rites of passage and personal milestones. The night sky becomes a backdrop for moments of reflection and transformation, marking significant changes in our lives. Whether it's a graduation, a marriage, or a personal achievement, the stars provide a sense of continuity and connection, reminding us of the larger narrative in which our individual stories are woven.

The process of personal growth often involves periods of darkness and uncertainty, much like navigating the night sky. The stars serve as beacons of hope and resilience, guiding us through these challenging times. By looking

CHAPTER 9: CELESTIAL BODIES AND PERSONAL GROWTH

to the stars, we find inspiration and strength, recognizing that even in the darkest moments, there is light to be found.

10

Chapter 10: The Therapeutic Power of Stargazing

Stargazing has long been recognized for its therapeutic benefits, offering a unique way to connect with the cosmos and find inner peace. This chapter delves into the psychological and emotional benefits of stargazing, exploring how it can be used as a tool for healing and personal well-being.

The act of stargazing encourages mindfulness and presence, allowing individuals to disconnect from the stresses of daily life and focus on the beauty of the night sky. This meditative practice can reduce anxiety and promote relaxation, fostering a sense of calm and tranquility. The stars provide a moment of respite, inviting us to pause and reflect on the vastness of the universe.

Stargazing also offers a unique perspective on our problems and challenges, helping us to see them in a broader context. The vastness of the cosmos reminds us of our small place within it, encouraging a sense of humility and perspective. This shift in perspective can be incredibly therapeutic, helping us to reframe our difficulties and approach them with a renewed sense of clarity and resilience.

In addition to its psychological benefits, stargazing can also foster a sense of connection and community. Sharing the experience of looking at the stars with others can create a sense of bonding and shared wonder, strengthening relationships and promoting social well-being. The stars become a common ground, bringing people together and fostering a sense of belonging.

11

Chapter 11: Celestial Archetypes and the Collective Unconscious

The concept of the collective unconscious, introduced by Carl Jung, explores the idea that certain symbols and archetypes are shared across cultures and time. The stars, with their universal presence and significance, serve as powerful archetypes within the collective unconscious. This chapter examines how celestial imagery influences our psychological landscape through these shared symbols.

Celestial archetypes, such as the hero's journey represented by the constellation Orion or the nurturing figure of the moon, resonate with our deepest psychological patterns. These symbols appear in myths, dreams, and art, reflecting fundamental aspects of the human experience. By examining these archetypes, we gain insights into our collective psyche and the universal themes that shape our lives.

The stars also serve as symbols of the eternal and the infinite, connecting us to the larger forces at play in the universe. This connection to the cosmos can evoke a sense of awe and wonder, fostering a deeper understanding of our place within the larger narrative. The celestial archetypes remind us of our interconnectedness and the shared journey of humanity.

The exploration of celestial archetypes and the collective unconscious offers valuable insights into our psychological landscape. By understanding the universal symbols that shape our thoughts and behaviors, we can navigate our inner worlds with greater awareness and clarity. The stars become a mirror to our collective psyche, reflecting the shared stories and experiences that unite us.

12

Chapter 12: The Future of Our Celestial Narrative

As we continue to explore the universe and expand our understanding of the cosmos, the celestial narrative will undoubtedly evolve. This final chapter explores the future of our relationship with the stars, considering how advancements in space exploration and technology will shape our psychological landscape.

The prospect of human settlement on other planets and the possibility of encountering extraterrestrial life offer new dimensions to our celestial narrative. These advancements challenge our understanding of identity, existence, and our place in the universe. The stars, once distant and untouchable, become destinations and neighbors, reshaping our psychological and cultural narratives.

The future of space exploration also raises questions about the ethical and environmental implications of our actions. As we reach for the stars, we must consider the impact of our endeavors on both the cosmos and our own planet. The celestial narrative becomes a call for responsible and sustainable exploration, reminding us of our interconnectedness with the universe.

Despite the uncertainties and challenges that lie ahead, our fascination with the stars remains unwavering. The celestial narrative continues to inspire and guide us, shaping our psychological landscape in profound ways. As we

CHAPTER 12: THE FUTURE OF OUR CELESTIAL NARRATIVE

look to the future, we are reminded of the enduring power of the stars and the stories they inspire, illuminating our journey through the cosmos and the human experience.

13

Chapter 13: Star Symbolism in Religion and Spirituality

The stars hold a significant place in religious and spiritual traditions across the world. This chapter explores the celestial symbolism found in various faiths and spiritual practices, highlighting the psychological impact of these cosmic connections. From the Star of Bethlehem in Christianity to the astrological significance in Hinduism, the stars serve as powerful symbols of divine guidance and enlightenment.

In many religions, the stars are seen as manifestations of the divine, representing the presence and power of higher beings. The night sky becomes a canvas for spiritual narratives, guiding believers in their faith and practice. These celestial symbols provide a sense of connection to the divine, offering comfort and inspiration in times of need.

Spiritual practices often involve rituals and meditations centered around the stars, harnessing their energy for personal growth and healing. The stars become a source of spiritual insight and transformation, guiding individuals on their paths to enlightenment. This chapter delves into the various ways in which celestial symbolism is integrated into spiritual traditions, shaping the psychological landscape of believers.

14

Chapter 14: The Role of Astronomy in Human Progress

Astronomy has played a crucial role in advancing human knowledge and understanding of the universe. This chapter examines the history of astronomical discoveries and their impact on our psychological and cultural development. From the heliocentric model proposed by Copernicus to the revolutionary findings of modern astrophysics, the study of the stars has continually reshaped our worldview.

The pursuit of astronomical knowledge has driven technological advancements and scientific progress. The development of telescopes, satellites, and space probes has expanded our understanding of the cosmos, revealing the intricate workings of celestial bodies. These discoveries have not only deepened our appreciation for the universe but have also inspired new narratives and ways of thinking.

The impact of astronomy on human progress extends beyond science and technology. The exploration of the stars has fueled our imagination and creativity, leading to new forms of art, literature, and cultural expression. This chapter explores the profound influence of astronomical discoveries on our psychological landscape, highlighting the interconnectedness of science, culture, and the human experience.

15

Chapter 15: The Future of Our Celestial Connection

As we look to the future, our connection to the stars will continue to evolve, driven by advancements in technology and exploration. This chapter envisions the possibilities and challenges that lie ahead, considering how our relationship with the cosmos will shape our psychological and cultural landscape.

The prospect of interstellar travel and the colonization of other planets presents both opportunities and ethical dilemmas. The stars, once distant and untouchable, may become our new homes, reshaping our understanding of identity, existence, and community. This chapter explores the potential impact of these developments on our collective psyche, as we navigate the unknown frontiers of space.

The future of our celestial connection also hinges on our responsibility to preserve and protect the cosmos. The ethical considerations of space exploration, such as the potential impact on extraterrestrial environments and the preservation of our own planet, become critical aspects of our celestial narrative. This chapter highlights the importance of mindful exploration, balancing our curiosity and ambition with respect for the universe.

The stars will undoubtedly continue to inspire and guide us, shaping our stories and our sense of self. As we embark on new adventures in the cosmos,

CHAPTER 15: THE FUTURE OF OUR CELESTIAL CONNECTION

we are reminded of the enduring power of the celestial narrative, illuminating our path and enriching our psychological landscape.

Book Description

"The Celestial Narrative, How Stars and Stories Shape Our Psychological Landscape" is a captivating exploration of the profound connection between the cosmos and the human psyche. Through twelve insightful chapters, this book delves into the rich tapestry of myths, legends, and scientific discoveries that have shaped our understanding of the stars and their impact on our psychological and cultural landscape.

From the ancient myths of constellations to the modern marvels of space exploration, "The Celestial Narrative" traces the evolution of our celestial fascination. It examines the symbolic power of the stars in art, literature, religion, and spirituality, highlighting their enduring influence on our emotions, dreams, and personal growth.

The book also explores the therapeutic benefits of stargazing, the role of celestial symbolism in dreams, and the impact of astronomical discoveries on human progress. Each chapter offers a unique perspective on the stars' role in shaping our collective and individual identities, weaving together historical insights, psychological theories, and cultural narratives.

"The Celestial Narrative" invites readers on a journey through the cosmos, encouraging them to reflect on their own connection to the stars and the stories that illuminate their lives. Whether you are a seasoned stargazer or simply curious about the mysteries of the night sky, this book offers a thought-provoking and inspiring exploration of the celestial and the terrestrial, reminding us of the timeless bond between the stars and our human experience.

www.ingramcontent.com/pod-product-compliance
Lightning Source LLC
LaVergne TN
LVHW020744090526
838202LV00057BA/6220